PRESENTED TO

BY

ON

Angels of the Bible

Illustrated by
Dennis Jones

Edited by
Catherine DeVries

■ ZondervanPublishingHouse
Grand Rapids, Michigan

Contents

Angels Stand Guard 8
Angel Helps Hagar and Ishmael . . . 10
Angel Talks to Abraham 12
Jacob Dreams About Angels 14
Angels Protect You 16
Angels Watch Over You 18
Angels Praise God 20
Angel in the Fire 22
Angel Shuts Lions' Mouths 24
Angel Gives Priest New Clothes . . . 26
Angel Appears to Zechariah 28
Angel Announces Jesus' Birth 30
Angels Worship Baby Jesus 32
Angel Appears to Shepherds 34
Angels Take Care of Jesus 36

Little Children's Angels 38
Angel Strengthens Jesus 40
Angel at Jesus' Tomb 42
Angels Talk to Mary Magdalene 44
Angel Visits Cornelius. 46
Angel Helps Peter Escape Prison . . . 48
Angel Comforts Paul. 50
Jesus Will Come With Angels 52
Angels Unaware 54
Angels Praise Jesus. 56
Angel Will Tell Everyone
    About God 58
Angel Shows Heaven to John. 60
Jesus Will Return ... With Angels! . . 62

Angels
Stand Guard

Genesis 3:23–24

The LORD God drove Adam and Eve out of the Garden of Eden. The LORD then placed angels on the east side of the Garden of Eden. He also placed a flaming sword there. It flashed back and forth. The angels and the sword guarded the way to the tree of life.

8

Angel Helps Hagar and Ishmael

Genesis 16:3–4; 21:10–12, 14–17, 19

Hagar had a son by Abraham. His name was Ishmael. Sarah told Abraham to send Hagar away with the boy. What Sarah said upset Abraham very much. But God told him to listen to her. So he gave Hagar and Ishmael food and a bottle of water. They wandered in the desert. When the water in the bottle was gone, Hagar put Ishmael under a bush. She began to sob.

Then the angel of God called out to Hagar from heaven. He said to her, "What is the matter? Do not be afraid." Then God opened Hagar's eyes. She saw a well of water. So she went and filled the bottle with water and gave Ishmael a drink.

Angel Talks to Abraham

Genesis 22:15, 17–18

The angel of the LORD called out to Abraham from heaven. The angel said that the LORD will bless Abraham and will make his children after him as many as the stars in the sky, as many as the grains of sand on the seashore. All nations on earth will be blessed because of Abraham's children. The angel said all of that would happen because Abraham obeyed the LORD.

Jacob Dreams About Angels

Genesis 28:10–13, 15

Jacob was traveling. He was far from home. He stopped for the night and lay down to sleep. In a dream he saw a stairway standing on the earth. Its top reached to heaven. The angels of God were going up and coming down on it. The LORD stood above the stairway. He said, "I am the LORD. I am with you. I will watch over you everywhere you go. And I will bring you back to this land. I will not leave you until I have done what I have promised you."

Angels Protect You

Psalm 34:4–5, 7

I looked to the LORD, and he answered me. He saved me from everything I was afraid of. Those who look to him beam with joy. They are never put to shame. The angel of the LORD stands guard around those who have respect for him. And he saves them.

Angels Watch Over You

Psalm 91:9, 11–12

The LORD is the one who keeps [you] safe. He will command his angels to take good care of you. They will lift you up in their hands.

Angels
Praise God

Psalm 103:20–21

Praise the LORD, you angels of his. Praise him, you mighty ones who carry out his orders and obey his word. Praise the LORD, all you angels in heaven. Praise him, all you who serve him and do what he wants.

Angel in the Fire

Daniel 3:12–13, 20–21, 25

Shadrach, Meshach and Abednego refused to worship gold statues and false gods. So King Nebuchadnezzar burned with anger. He ordered them to be thrown into a really hot furnace. The three men were tied up. And they were thrown into the furnace. Then the king said, "Look! I see four men walking around in the fire. They aren't tied up. And the fire hasn't even harmed them. The fourth man looks like an angel, a son of the gods!"

Angel Shuts Lions' Mouths

Daniel 6:13, 16, 21–22

Daniel prayed to God three times every day. But this was against the rules of King Darius. So the king gave the order. Daniel was thrown into the lions' den. God sent an angel. The angel shut the mouths of the lions. "They haven't hurt me at all," said Daniel to the king. That's because Daniel trusted in God.

Angel Gives Priest New Clothes

Zechariah 3:3–7

Jeshua was a high priest. He stood in front of an angel. Jeshua was wearing clothes that were very dirty. The angel spoke to those who were standing near him. He said, "Take his dirty clothes off." Then he said to Jeshua, "I have taken your sin away. I will put fine clothes on you."

So the people dressed him in new clothes while the angel of the LORD stood by. Then the angel spoke to Jeshua. He said, "The LORD who rules over all says, 'You must live the way I want you to. And you must do what I want you to do. Then you will rule in my temple.'"

Angel Appears to Zechariah

Luke 1:11–14, 19

An angel of the Lord appeared to Zechariah inside the temple of the Lord. Zechariah was amazed and terrified. But the angel said to him, "Do not be afraid. Your prayer has been heard. Your wife Elizabeth will have a child. It will be a boy, and you must name him John. His birth will make many people very glad.

"I am Gabriel. I serve God. I have been sent to speak to you and to tell you this good news."

Angel Announces Jesus' Birth

Luke 1:26–28, 30–33

God sent the angel Gabriel to Nazareth, a town in Galilee. He was sent to a virgin named Mary. Mary was engaged to a man named Joseph. The angel greeted her and said, "Do not be afraid, Mary. God is very pleased with you. You will become pregnant and give birth to a son. You must name him Jesus. He will be great and will be called the Son of the Most High God. He will rule forever over his people. His kingdom will never end."

Angels Worship Baby Jesus

Luke 2:6–7; Hebrews 1:6

While Joseph and Mary were in Bethlehem, the time came for Jesus to be born. Mary gave birth and wrapped Jesus in large strips of cloth. Then she placed him in a manger.

When God brought Jesus into the world, God said, "Let all of [my] angels worship him." God's first and only Son is over all things.

Angel Appears to Shepherds

Luke 2:8–12, 15

Some shepherds were looking after their sheep in a field. An angel of the Lord appeared to them. And the glory of the Lord shone around them. They were terrified. But the angel said to them, "Do not be afraid. I bring you good news of great joy. Today in the town of David a Savior has been born to you. He is Christ the Lord. Here is how you will know I am telling you the truth. You will find a baby wrapped in strips of cloth and lying in a manger." Then the shepherds said to one another, "Let's go to Bethlehem. Let's see this thing that has happened, which the Lord has told us about."

Angels Take Care of Jesus

Matthew 4:8–11

The devil took Jesus to a very high mountain. He showed Jesus all the kingdoms of the world and their glory. "If you bow down and worship me," he said, "I will give you all of this." Jesus said to him, "Get away from me, Satan! It is written, 'Worship the Lord your God. He is the only one you should serve.'" Then the devil left Jesus. Angels came and took care of him.

Little Children's Angels

Matthew 18:5, 10–11

Jesus said, "Anyone who welcomes a little child like this in my name welcomes me. See that you don't look down on one of these little ones. Their angels in heaven can go at any time to see my Father who is in heaven."

38

Angel Strengthens Jesus

Luke 22:39–44

Jesus went to the Mount of Olives. His disciples followed him. When they reached the place, Jesus went a short distance away from them. There he got down on his knees and prayed. He said, "Father, if you are willing, take this cup of suffering away from me. But do what you want, not what I want."

An angel from heaven appeared to Jesus and gave him strength. Because he was very sad and troubled, Jesus prayed even harder.

Angel at Jesus' Tomb

Matthew 28:2–3, 5–6

There was a powerful earthquake. An angel of the Lord came down from heaven. He went to Jesus' tomb, rolled back the stone and sat on it. The angel's body shone like lightning. His clothes were as white as snow.

The angel said to the women nearby, "Don't be afraid. I know that you are looking for Jesus, who was crucified. He is not here! He has risen, just as he said he would!"

Angels Talk
to Mary Magdalene

John 20:11–14, 16

Mary stood outside the tomb crying. As she cried, she bent over to look into the tomb. She saw two angels dressed in white. They were seated where Jesus' body had been. They asked her, "Woman, why are you crying?"

"They have taken my Lord away," she said. "I don't know where they have put him." Then she turned around and saw Jesus standing there. Jesus said to her, "Mary."

Angel Visits Cornelius

Acts 10:1–5, 42–43

Cornelius was a Roman commander. He and all his family were faithful and worshiped God. He gave freely to people who were in need. He prayed to God regularly. One day an angel of God came to him and said, "Cornelius!" Cornelius was afraid. He stared at the angel.

"What is it, Lord?" he asked. The angel answered, "Your prayers and gifts to poor people have come up like an offering to God. So he has remembered you." The angel told Cornelius to send for the disciple Peter to help spread God's Word to all people.

Angel Helps Peter Escape Prison

Acts 12:4, 6–8, 10–11

King Herod arrested Peter and put him in prison. Peter was sleeping between two soldiers. Two chains held him there. Lookouts stood guard at the entrance. Suddenly an angel of the Lord appeared. A light shone in the prison cell. The angel woke Peter up and said, "Quick! Get up!" The chains fell off Peter's wrists.

Then the angel said to him, "Follow me." They passed the guards and came to the iron gate leading to the city. It opened for them by itself. They went through it. Suddenly the angel left Peter. Then Peter realized what had happened. He said, "Now I know for sure that the Lord sent his angel. He set me free."

Angel Comforts Paul

Acts 27:22–24

Paul's ship was caught in a storm. Paul said to the men on the ship, "Now I beg you to be brave. Not one of you will die. Only the ship will be destroyed. I belong to God and serve him. Last night his angel stood beside me. The angel said, 'Do not be afraid, Paul. God has shown his grace by sparing the lives of all those sailing with you.'"

Jesus Will Come With Angels

2 Thessalonians 1:6–7

God is fair. He will pay back trouble to those who give you trouble. He will help you who are troubled. All of those things will happen when the Lord Jesus appears from heaven. He will come in blazing fire. He will come with the angels who are given the power to do what God wants.

Angels Unaware

Hebrews 13:1–2

Keep on loving each other as brothers. Don't forget to welcome strangers. By doing that, some people have welcomed angels without knowing it.

Angels Praise Jesus

Revelation 5:11–12

Millions and millions of angels surrounded the throne. In a loud voice they sang, "The Lamb is worthy! He is worthy to receive power and wealth and wisdom and strength! He is worthy to receive honor and glory and praise!"

Angel Will Tell Everyone About God

Revelation 14:6–7

An angel will tell everyone on earth the good news that will always be true. He will tell it to every nation, tribe, language and people. He will say, "Have respect for God. Give him glory. Worship him who made the heavens and the earth."

Angel Shows Heaven
to John

Revelation 22:1, 5

The angel showed John heaven. He showed him the river of the water of life. It was as clear as crystal. It flowed from the throne of God and of the Lamb. There will be no more night. God's people will not need the light of a lamp or the light of the sun. The Lord God will give them light. They will rule for ever and ever.

Jesus Will Return ... With Angels!

Matthew 24:30–31

Someday Jesus will come back. He will be coming on the clouds of the sky with power and great glory. He will send his angels with a loud trumpet call. They will gather his chosen people from many places on the earth. They will bring them from one end of the heavens to the other.

Project Management and Editorial: **Catherine DeVries**
Interior Art and Cover Art: **Dennis Jones**
Interior Design: **Sue Vandenberg Koppenol**
Cover Design: **Jody Langley**
Printing: **Quebecor Printing, Kingsport, TN**